Release Me

by

Linda G. Barrett

Illustrations by Giana Bisceglia

Release Me

by

Linda G. Barrett

Copyright © 2019 Linda G. Barrett

All rights reserved. No part of this book may be reproduced in any form or by any electronic or mechanical means, including information storage and retrieval systems, without permission in writing from the publisher, except by a reviewer who may quote brief passages in a review.

Printed in the United States of America

Illustrator: Giana Bisceglia
Editor: Karin Nicely (Writing Nicely)
Designer: Julie Glynn (New Eden Graphics)
Cover photographer: John Carpenter

First Printing, 2019

ISBN-13: 978-1-7331737-0-4

Linda Barrett
sacredcircle650@gmail.com

Dedication

Dedicated to the seekers aching for release from their pain and wanting someone to hear their cries.

Table of Contents

Take My Hand 7

Two Souls Wanting 8

Cufflinks 9

The Lies of Childhood 10

The Master's Vengeance is Complete 12

Madness and Loving to Death 13

I Feel You No More 14

I Didn't Want You 16

Wicked Laughter 17

Whispers Without Words 18

The Parchment Is Finally Heard 20

Tribute 21

Release Me 22

The Lost Unfinished Writing 24

The Pain is Deep and So Is the Journey 25

Whisper You Love Me 26

Promises Made 28

Soul's Desire Released 30

Before I Awake 31

I Remember 32

Ripples of Passion 33

Stardust of Your Soul 34

Cathedrals of Time 36

Is It You or Me That I Hear? 37

Silent Screams 38

A Fitting End 39

Epilogue 41

Where the Inspiration Comes From 43

Acknowledgements 45

Bio 47

Take My Hand

Those who proclaim love only have self-need
Their own pain to escape from
With nothing left to give away

Desperately alone
Old shoes no longer fit
Angry, bitter, sad, dejected, hurt
Wanting to be seen. Noticed. Desired. Wanted.

Can't anyone hear me?

I wear my masquerade
Watching the fringes of life
Walking the tightrope of sanity
Wanting to live but standing in the shadow of hopelessness
A lost soul waiting at the brink of the veil
Will anyone notice if I'm gone?

They have their own pain to escape from
I'm just another lost soul

Please
Take my hand

Two Souls Wanting

I remember your all-consuming need and fire
Just the thought of me could make you weak
You stirred that fire within me as well
Even now

When we were together, nothing else existed
Both consumed with each other
That was enough
Then

Your appetite for others to share your bed
Too hard to look away from
Even though you always return to me
Your heart belongs to another

Two souls wanting
My tears have grown weary of falling
My cheeks forever wet
How I long to be your one

I cannot undo the sins of others
The betrayals done to you
Your mind, body, and soul want peace

You always return to me
Resting your head upon my breast
Your tears falling
Your cheeks forever wet
Two souls wanting
How I long to be your one

I see the sadness in your eyes
The despair behind your smile
No matter the pleasures we share
Your heart belongs to another
You forsake all others
Abandoned your dreams
And now you walk your road alone
How I long to be your one

I wish you could see the sadness in my eyes
The despair behind my smile
That I am walking your road with you

Two souls wanting

How I long to be your one

Cufflinks

Veiled away from judging eyes
I give myself completely
Soul and body
Sharing an all-consuming hunger

Sharp nails slowly slice pearl buttons from your shirt
Cufflinks fall silently to the floor
The shadows of candlelight dance on your face, stirring my restrained desire
Your eyes shine with fire and need
I feel the warmth and firmness of your hands as they settle on my hips
As you pull me in tight against you

The tone of your voice, so deep
Its vibrations sending tremors down my body
Breathing in your rich-scented imported cologne
Savoring it
Like fine wine rolling over the tongue
Your taste remembered

I take in a deep breath and open my eyes
You're gone

My eyes desperately search the room
Was it only a dream?
Too often do we meet like this

As I slowly move across the floor
Holding myself for comfort and allowing my tears to flow freely
A glint of light catches my eye
And I bend down to pick up your cufflinks

The Lies of Childhood

The lies of childhood
Stories continue in life
If there is a God
I've been forgotten
A life of solitude
Standing within many

Love fleeting
Happiness scarce
Heart broken and bleeding

It hurts to be forgotten
Just wanting to be loved

The Master's Vengeance Is Complete

The wrath of fire ignites from the core
Sparked by the betrayal of the Master
Secrets and intimate moments shared with lovers outside of the sanctuary
Breaking our core of silence and trust
Your known lies told to meet your own selfish desires
Heard by the Watchers

Your punishment by the Master will be complete
Flesh torn from the bone as you desperately writhe to free yourself from the tight shackles that bind you
Shrieks of terror and pain go unheard by the executioner
Tortured to the brink of death
Enough life left to allow your memory of decisions
Your lovers, forced to watch
Their secrets with you will be forever burned into their silence
As they watch you torn and bitten by the Master
His screaming growls of fury as he slashes you with his long sharp nails and bites deep into your meat
Tearing your flesh from itself
Hearing your terror-filled wails and pleas for mercy
Or death

The vengeance of the Master is unquestioned and complete
Your sworn allegiance was forever, a commitment made in blood
Now your blood spills to the brink of death

If you're allowed to live, the Master will mark you for all to see your betrayal to him and his punishment
Forever marked, an eternity of retribution, of slavery to the Master
Or death

Decide, whispers the Master as he leans in, close to your ear, feeling his heavy, hot breath
Thick with the smell of your own blood

Decide…

You barely whisper,
Death

With a howl and scream, the Master bites and rips out your throat
Leaving an unrecognizable mass of blood, bones, and tissue

The Master's vengeance is complete

Madness and Loving to Death

I see you
Watching again
Second sight sees you well
Why do we run?
Words of melody, fire, and loving
To death
The Darker side of Light
These powers are indeed inviting
Eleven candles burning
The air thick with incense
My senses blurring and my heart beating hard
My hands trembling
Why am I to meet you only here
Where I feel alive and I see power
My power from before
Long before the Light
Or after?
It's still here
And I begin to dance
The thoughts of madness
Growing tired of living a parallel world
Separate, together, separate again
The duplicity continues into madness
Daily actions with words spoken into dead air
I can only see the shadows of people
Great Spirit, the Skulls, the Fire watching me
I'm tired of living in lifelessness
I want to feel
Again

I Feel You No More

You stand before me
My finger to your lips
I look deep into your eyes
Seeing your deceit
My lips curve in a dangerous smile
My eyes fill with fury

I once had a heart of tenderness
But my favorite Knight
Has forgotten his manners

Our eyes stay locked
You cannot look away
Fear creeps into your soul
You think to break free
But you know if you move
You'll be torn apart

You are so beautiful
I lean against you one last time
I feel your warmth
Your tension
Remembering your gentleness of touch

Between breaths
1001 of my Knights appear and surround us
My sworn protectors
You know how well they're trained
How loyal they are to me

Don't be in a hurry to die for honor
And your place in heaven
My love
Heaven might not exist

For the last time
I outline your lips with my tongue
I circle around you
I feel the whole of your body
Within my hands
My eyes close in beautiful memory

Your master did not train you well
He will need to be reminded
Who his master is
He will not be let off as easily as you
Some lessons must be burned into the soul
To be remembered

I turn my back to you and walk away
My Knights break their circle
To allow me to pass through
Then close again behind me
Their formation tightens
Moving in closer to you

Living with dishonor is worse than death

I walk far beyond the circle
My face still turned away
I can feel your rapid heartbeat
I sense your eyes widen
I hear your muffled scream

Then

Silence

I feel you

No more

I Didn't Want You

Thoughts overheard
Wanting to be the choice
You veil your eyes as you watch me
Lips sealed to silence

You remember who I really am
I've forgotten
Hidden from myself

I didn't want you

I remember your words whispered
Memorized for eternity
Breathed into form

Fragments of self left
Choosing to forget
I turn so memory won't be summoned
I don't see you there
In the shadows

I didn't want you

Would you come for me
Fight for me
Remember me

Do I dare speak your name
To bring you back
Wanting to be held by you once more
If I open my arms
Will you return
Again

Wasted linen and lace
Shadows fading
Broken hearts
Your memory
Let it fade from my soul

Would you come for me
Fight for me
Remember me

I want you

Wicked Laughter

Deviant behavior
Fueled by lust
Dance of the demons

Screams not heard
Thrills of the flesh
Roll down the spine
And flow over the skin
Like honey
Slow and thick

Skin pierced and hung
Exquisite ecstasy

Wicked laughter
Token lust
I'm the one
You can't trust

Scream for me

As you feel
Skin splits open
Beneath the claws
The scent of fresh blood

In ecstasy
You can't let go
The rapture's coming

You can't let go

Whispers Without Words

All your women wear your mark
Just the touch of it allows flooding of memories and ecstasy
I don't want to be one of so many
The exquisite pain
Is it worth it?

You walk slowly towards me
The others disappear now
Just you
Just me
My soul stands naked before your eyes
Layers of sin peel away
Your eyes, so beautiful and deep
I see reflections of our past lives
We've been here for a long time

I take another mark from you
The blade is offered again
How many times must I endure?
I find the blade in my hand
The light shines off the sharp edge
I slowly glide the flat side against my skin
So soft and quiet

The whispers begin again
Do I dare listen?
Can you hear them, or are they yours?
The light fades as I begin to listen
Whispers without words
I feel an unfamiliar strength of old
You smile, slowly disappearing into the shadows
The air now has a frequency and a vibration of its own
And I carry the black feathers and the wings of the Dark Angel

You stand before me
You show yourself to me
The blade is offered to you
You smile and touch my mark that's now yours to carry
Your soul stands naked before my eyes

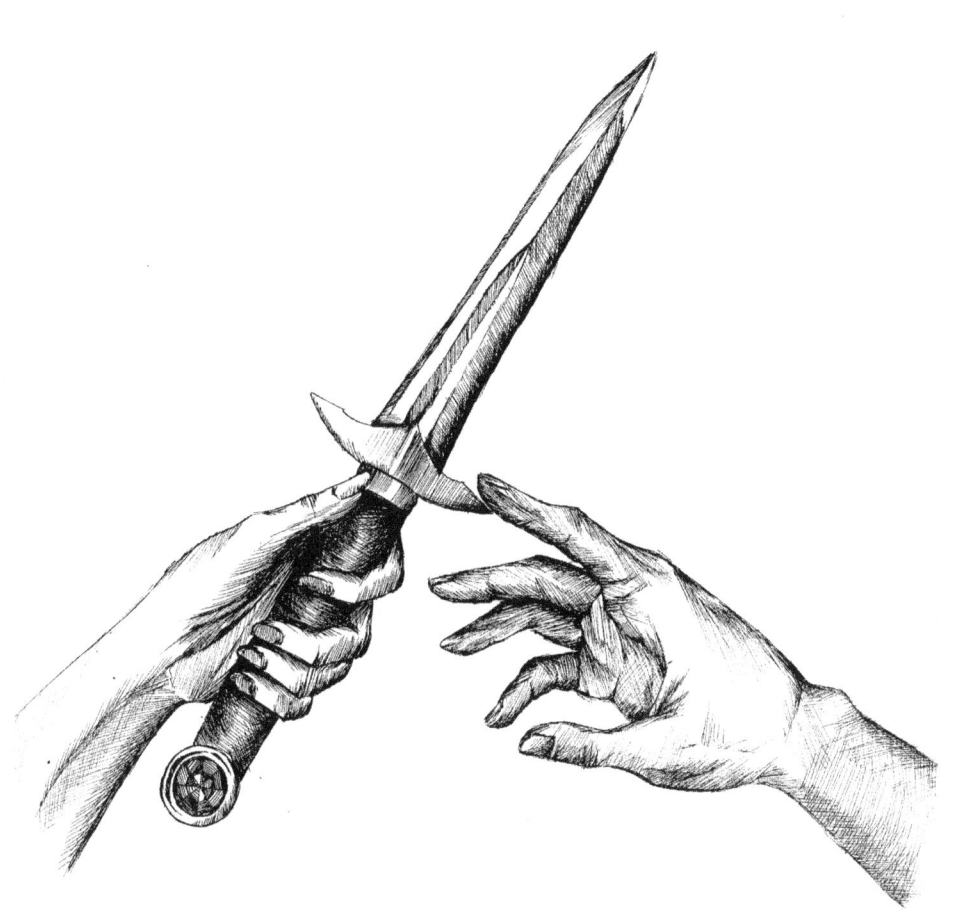

The Parchment Is Finally Heard

The voices of the mind are unrelenting
Like fountain-pen ink flowing like blood
Touched to dry, blank parchment
Seeping quickly through the fibers
Searching for its purpose

Fervent prayers fall on a deaf soul
Words crying out to be heard
Our yearnings are old
"You're not like the rest," is whispered to me
Layers of defense begin falling to the ground
As the ancient voices now are heard

My fingers touch the dry parchment
As the blood-ink flows across the page
The hidden words converge into their destined design
Allowing themselves to be seen
Their ancient wisdom giving profound strength
Validation of my own destiny
The voices of the mind beginning to still
Finding peace as the parchment's words are finally heard

Tribute

The child lost
Grows and lives beyond the veil
Giving strength

Her voice through the hushed whispers of darkness

A fleeting wisp of her essence in candle smoke
A shadow within the mist

Release Me

Has my time drawn near?
The veil is thinner now
If my soul has not been mine
Why then the pain of redemption?
You watch without speaking
But I hear the whispers of the demons of old
With every memory, my heart hurts more and my despair deepens
What deed was done, so deep to make me touch the darkness with such
    knowing but yet so much
Strength to defend so many?
I'm losing the light
The despair too dark
Just this side of the veil
You stand watching
On the other side
I see your slow smile
The battle has been so long

I want to feel again
My breath to catch again

They think they know me
Why won't you release me?
The robes I carry, beneath and concealing, have become too heavy
Release me
Or love me

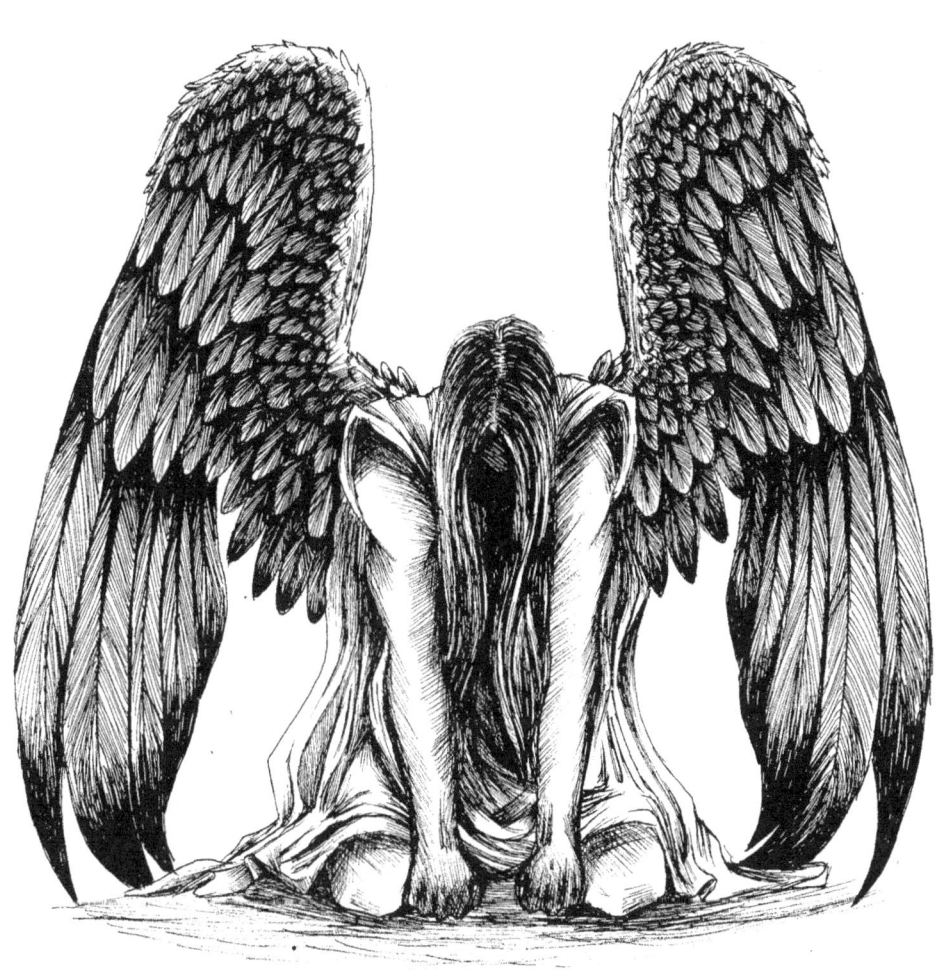

The Lost Unfinished Writing

The spell is cast
I see your smile—or is it mine?
The soul SCREAMS
The mind fights and the stomach tightens as the body shakes
The tone awaits the memory
Where are you? Or can't you do anything but watch?
The tone is calling
It's not gentle anymore as patience wanes
I feel the full arena
I'm choking
Are you real? Or am I just insane?

I feel the cracking of the mantle
I see my shield
It's too close to the surface now
The shell is splitting
From this day forward, for richer or poorer, till death…

I call on the fire
I feel the wave of enchantment
I take in an old breath
And I'm calmer now

The Pain is Deep and So Is the Journey

You stand a silent watch
Solitude and wanting to share
Silent vigil, Sentry of Time

Lips, firm and closed, do not speak
Yet Wisdom speaks with eyes of knowing
The mind wanders but the heart hears and knows the Truth
The pain is deep and so is the journey

The grid is set, my protection mantle near, my white spirit with me…in me…
    with me
I feel my feather settle upon me
They know my heart and watch
You stand, silent, and watch my confusion
You stand with angels near
But your eyes stay fixed and your lips stay still
Your gaze shifts and your eyes see mine
Your breastplate shines with a burst of light
And beneath I see the light in your heart
Your eyes stay fixed, your mouth stays silent
The hearts touch and the healing begins
The pain is deep and so is the journey

I see the fields of Light
And I begin to remember…
Hear the notes and see them turn fluid
Feel them wash over the soul
And see the Light begin to open
Hear the song of Spirit and let me remember
I see your familiar face
But you're not here
The clouds gather
But the storm parts
The music soothes and my Spirit cries
The pain is deep and so is the journey

Touch my face as you touch my heart
Wipe away my tears, for they are old
The journey is deep and so is the pain

Do you know my heart?

Whisper You Love Me

I catch a glimpse of you
An accidental meeting
Memory floods back
Time and distance between us disappear

A smoke-filled nightclub
A micro-mini black velvet skirt
High spiked heels
The sailboat
My man in uniform

There are many different types of addiction
You were mine

The voices warned me, but your scent overwhelmed me

I now stand frozen, not trusting myself to move
I pretend to listen to conversations around me
But can only hear my own pulse

We totally gave ourselves to each other
Without restraint
No inhibitions

I want to taste you again
I close my eyes to steady my breath
Knees weak
Trembling inside

Memory of your whispers of
"I'm sorry"
Your sense of duty keeping us apart
The nights that turned into days and back into nights
"I love you"
Whispers
Believed
Yours and mine

I feel your arms slide around my waist
I turn as you pull me in tight
You whisper
"I'm here now. I'm yours."
"I love you."
Whispers told again
Yours and mine
Believed

Promises Made

Black candles burning
The promise of lace and pressed white linen
Your gift of persuasion, intense and unmasked
Stolen moments
Straining from secret desires and hidden glances
Our time now always concealed
I breathe in your intoxicating, heady scent
You lightly touch my shoulder with skilled hands
Your fingers caress my skin, arousing familiar sensuous responses

Promises made
Remembered
Broken

Tight embrace
Your breath on the back of my neck
The touch of lust consumes

More promises made
Known to be broken
Your scent remains

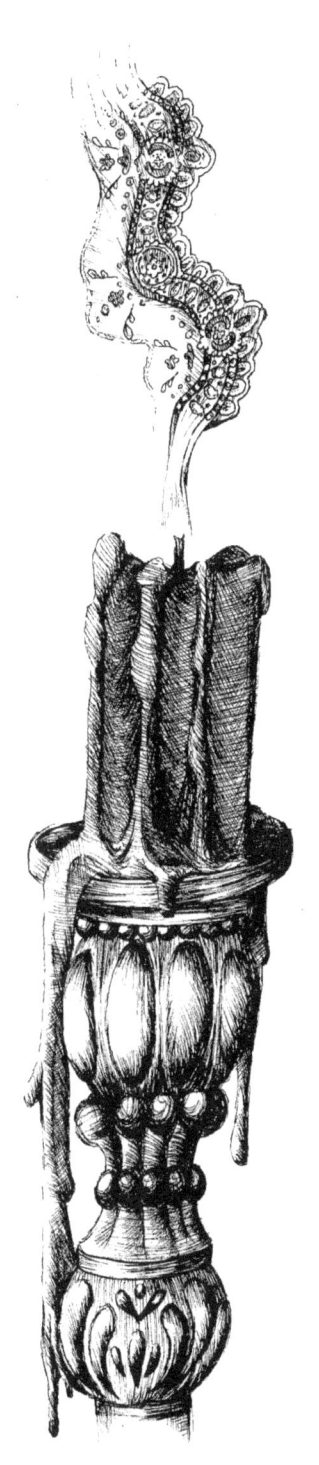

Soul's Desire Released

The desperate desire of the soul
Scratching and clawing
Begging to be released
Too close to the surface now
Can no longer be contained

The body no longer wanting to hold them back
Silent screams have been swallowed too long

A prisoner of righteousness
Self-deprived
Confined by private thoughts
Virtue for the sake of
Misguided honor and morality

The flesh begins to shudder and shake
And it thrills to the response
Heavy thunder in the background grows closer
Skies darken
The storm opens as fear grips the soul

Unrestrained movement
Thrashing uncontrollably
As the mind's matrix of creation
Fights the destined metamorphosis
Back into its sanity

The sky ablaze with lightning
Illuminating the flowing tears, quickening pulse, gnashing teeth
Writhing anguish of releasing screams of
Unfathomable pain from muscles, blood, and tissue
Sweat dripping from fingertips, face, and breasts

The body trembles and is rebirthed into its true beast

Leaving the soul naked
A final Genesis of released desires

Before I Awake

Before I awake
I feel you between heartbeats
Whispers of a kiss
The mist softly speaks my name that left upon a breath
So gently
From so far away
Echoes of words dissipate into the fog and settle into my heart
The dance is slowing
Before I remember to forget
I feel you between heartbeats
Whispers of a kiss

I Remember

She catches my scent
And slowly she turns toward me with a smile
As the light glints from her eyes
The memory of her bite flows over me like honey
My senses heighten
Visions wave in and out, over and around me
My passion is instantly painful
But I'm weak with desire
Entangled within the vines in the shadows
Sharp nails slowly move down my back

Voices, whispers
Breathless
Delicious
Screams
Racing heart
Why can't I move?
I open my eyes and she's gone
I remain breathless in memory
Her bite, her glinting fire
Forever emblazed behind my closed eyes
I remember

Ripples of Passion

Ripples of passion awaken the soul
Do I continue to fight the demons or finally succumb and be condemned?
Desire, passion, regret
Touch, essence, taste
I awake

Stardust of Your Soul

I stand firm
Sword drawn
Eyes fixed
I've found my target
Judgment and penance have come for you
My grip holds the ripples of your strangled cries for mercy

Like acid on a wing
Felt but not heard

With lightning speed, I pierce your heart
Your soul explodes
The demon is released but held in check
The stardust of your soul settles
With stillness finally found

I stand firm
Eyes fixed
The stardust of my soul settles
With stillness finally found

Cathedrals of Time

Cathedrals of Time with dolphin protection
Chords of sound, the melody enchanting
Touching, uplifting
Fluid beauty

I can hear the flames
And they speak of purity
If you never knew the Darkness, how would you know the Light?

Thoughts provoke and visions travel
I know your eyes
I know you're near
Shape shift and I can see
For now my eyes are yours

With our breath I feel your knowing
And I see your light
We travel forever in a moment
Together but separate
Do you remember?
We've shared the Light
Do you remember?
Cross the threshold and become Light

As you were is gone
As you will be is here

The flute still sings
And the feather still flies
Do you remember your Light?
The mood shifts and the light changes
Was it yours or mine?

The circle of light calls me back
The light separates
As it does, it expands

Think of me and touch the Light
Hearts become one…two…one
I miss you

Is It You or Me That I Hear?

Is it you or me that I hear?
I feel the dance before I hear the music
The familiar yet distant, drumming rhythm
There are others, but I am alone
Within my own dance
I dance through my soul and see old lives
Was it really that long ago?
The steps are an old memory
I feel the power build with each footfall
The tempo rises as does my spirit

Spinning and spinning

I laugh as I feel the Dark Angel return
The force is still there, and I tremble
The spark ignites, and I no longer feel the ground
The fire explodes, and I feel free
The music flows over, around, through me

Spinning and spinning

I see the faces of prior battles, enemies still held in check
The power is returning, the decision made
The spinning stops, but the music remains
As I again feel the ground under my feet
The notes change, and I now can hear the whispers of old
The music quiets, but the power remains
The Dark Angel stands before me, within me, before me
In me

Silent Screams

The flame rises between vibrations of life
Silent screams
Love so deep
Unbearable heartache
Denied desires
Is my road to insanity complete?
Images and voices unspoken endure
Your lying smile
Destined to feel but not to know
Haunting memory with silent, anguished tears
Not seen. Not heard. Not felt.

The piercing and burning of flesh
Release me to feel
Something

A Fitting End

I stand at the mountaintop
As the ground shakes under my feet
Or is it just me shaking like thunder?
I did not expect you to find me here
I am not prepared for you
Or was that your intention?

My heart broken
Memory of my sacrifice
Your abandonment

How did you know I was meeting my angel here?
I can no longer bear the pain
Tears gone
Empty now

My angel is close

I feel your heart
I see your tears
You reach for me
And finally hold me

I feel your angel is near
Mine and yours together

A fitting end
Or is it the beginning
Again…

Epilogue

"Sometimes you need to live a life alone in order to be able to listen and to hear Spirit. It can be good to have a heart that has had sorrow and pain so there is room for it to fill with the right thing to do when the time comes to do it."
–The Morrigan

"…we are never really alone. At most we can be private, but even then, we are part of each other and of Spirit."
–Heidi

The Hopi say that the Great Spirit gives us tragedy and heartache so we do not forget the power we carry and do not forget to ask for help.

To experience the Darkness is to know and embrace the Light.

Dance barefoot in the rain.
Hug a tree.
Listen to the stillness.
Trust yourself.
You can survive life.

Where the Inspiration Comes From

I've been asked where these poem ideas come from. The words come as I journey in lucid meditation. What that means is I'm fully awake while traveling in a meditative state within my mind's eye.

I always listen to music during this process, and I have found that, for me, music within the lower rhythmic tones and certain vibrations allows for spontaneous writing. As I listen to a piece of music, I don't hear the words but rather feel the emotion and tones of the music, and I continue to repeat that piece until the journey has completed itself.

The words flow to paper, but they are veiled and forgotten to me until I come out of the journey.

Every poem is true in that I experience every story—each emotion, every discovery, all the pain and heartache. The people and events are real. They may not all be here, present in our vibration, but they are real in theirs.

The veil is real.

Acknowledgements

I would like to give my profound gratitude and sincere thank you to my editor, Karin Nicely. Without her encouragement, insight, and patience, this book would never have happened. I am deeply and truly grateful.

To my BFF: thank you for your never-ending support, for walking my road of joy with me, and for helping me find my voice.

To W and N: I love you more.

A special thank you to Ute for allowing me to honor her amazing mother, my Shamanic teacher and friend, Heidi.

Bio

Linda lives in North Central Florida with her husband, two dogs, and three cats. All rescued. Except the husband. Well, maybe him, too.

sacredcircle650@gmail.com

www.ingramcontent.com/pod-product-compliance
Lightning Source LLC
Chambersburg PA
CBHW052037070526
44584CB00020B/3145